Find & Speak
FRENCH Words

Louise Millar

Illustrations by Louise Comfort
French adviser: Marie-Thérèse Bougard

b small publishing
www.bsmall.co.uk

À la ferme

Look for these words in the big picture.

le cheval
ler sh-val

la vache
lah vash

le chien
ler shee-yah

Can you find another cat somewhere in the book?

la souris
lah soo-ree

2

On the farm

le cochon
ler coh-shoh

le mouton
ler moo-toh

le canard
ler can-ar

le chat
ler shah

Say the French word aloud.

la chèvre
lah shevr

3

Dans la salle de classe

la maîtresse
lah met-<u>ress</u>

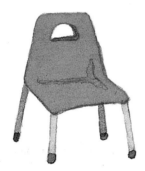

la chaise
lah shez

la table
lah tabl'

le crayon de couleur
ler cray-<u>oh</u> der cool-err

4

In the classroom

le livre
ler leevr'

la colle
lah koll

l'ordinateur
lordeenat-err

le stylo
ler stee<u>lo</u>

le papier
ler papee-<u>eh</u>

Say the French word aloud.

Ton corps

Look for these words in the big picture.

Count the number of children at the party.

la tête
lah tet

les yeux
lez-yer

le nez
ler neh

la bouche
lah boosh

6

Your body

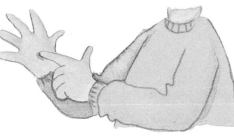

la main
lah mah

la jambe
lah shahmb

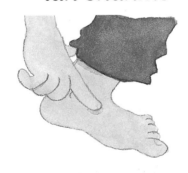

le pied
ler pee-<u>eh</u>

les épaules
lezeh-<u>pol</u>

Say the French word aloud.

le bras
ler brah

7

Les couleurs dans la jungle

Look for these words in the big picture.

rouge
rooshj

bleu/bleue
bl'/bl'

How many purple things are in the scene?

vert/verte
vair/vairt

jaune
shown

8

Colours in the jungle

blanc/blanche
bloh/blonsh

violet/violette
veeoh-<u>leh</u>/veeoh-<u>let</u>

marron
mah-<u>roh</u>

orange
oranshj

noir/noire
nwah/nwah

Say the French word aloud.

9

Le coffre à déguisements

Look for these words in the big picture.

la jupe
lah shoop

la robe
lah rob

Find someone on another page wearing a hat.

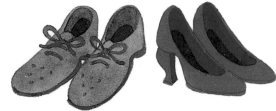

les chaussures
leh showss-yoor

Say the French word aloud.

The dressing-up box

le pantalon
leh pantah-<u>loh</u>

la chemise
lah sher-<u>meez</u>

le manteau
ler man<u>to</u>

les chaussettes
leh show-<u>set</u>

le chapeau
ler shap<u>o</u>

le pyjama
ler peeshah-<u>mah</u>

Au zoo

Look for these words in the big picture.

la girafe
lah jeer<u>aff</u>

le lion
ler lee<u>oh</u>

le tigre
ler teegr'

le crocodile
ler kroko<u>deel</u>

Find another animal in the book that could be in the zoo.

12

At the zoo

l'éléphant
lelay<u>foh</u>

l'ours blanc
loors bloh

l'hippopotame
leepopo<u>tam</u>

le serpent
ler sair<u>poh</u>

Say the French word aloud.

le dauphin
ler doh-<u>fah</u>

13

Le transport

Look for these words in the big picture.

l'autobus
low-toh-<u>boos</u>

l'arrêt d'autobus
lar<u>reh</u> dow-toh-<u>boos</u>

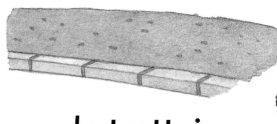

le trottoir
ler trot<u>wah</u>

Find a car somewhere else in the book.

la rue
lah roo

Transport

les feux
leh fer

la bicyclette
lah beesee-klet

la voiture
lah vwot-yoor

le camion
ler kamee-oh

Say the French word aloud.

la voiture de police
lah vwot-yoor der polees

À la plage

la mouette
lah moo-et

le poisson
ler pwahssoh

le coquillage
ler kokeeah-sh

la mer
lah mair

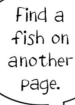

At the beach

l'algue
lalg

le rocher
ler rosh<u>eh</u>

le voilier
ler vwalee-<u>eh</u>

le sable
ler sabl'

Say the French word aloud.

la vague
lah vag

Ma famille

Look for these words in the big picture.

mon frère
moh frair

ma sœur
mah sir

mon père
moh pair

ma mère
mah mair

How many people are in your family?

My family

mon oncle
moh onkl'

ma tante
mah tohnt

ma grand-mère
mah groh-<u>mair</u>

mes cousins
meh koo<u>zah</u>

mon grand-père
moh groh-<u>pair</u>

Say the French word aloud.

19

C'est la fête

le sandwich
ler sond<u>weech</u>

la glace
lah glas

le gâteau
ler g<u>atoh</u>

les frites
leh freet

Party time

la boisson gazeuse
lah bwasoh gaz<u>erz</u>

le jus d'orange
ler shoo d'o<u>ronsh</u>

l'eau
loh

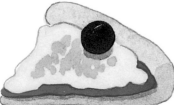

la pizza
lah peet-<u>sah</u>

le chocolat
ler shoko<u>lah</u>

Say the French word aloud.

21

Acheter des jouets

Look for these words in the big picture.

les perles
leh pairl

le robot
le roh-<u>boh</u>

le puzzle
ler pooz-<u>leh</u>

Find a teddy bear in another scene.

le baby-foot
ler baby-<u>foot</u>

Shopping for toys

Say the French word aloud.

la balle
lah bal

le jeu
ler sher

le jeu-vidéo
ler sher veedeh-<u>oh</u>

la maquette d'avion
lah ma<u>ket</u> davee-<u>oh</u>

le nounours
ler noo-<u>noorss</u>

Dans la cuisine

Look for these words in the big picture.

le frigo
ler free-<u>goh</u>

le verre
ler vair

la casserole
lah kasse<u>rol</u>

Find a glass on another page.

le couteau
ler koo<u>toh</u>

In the kitchen

l'assiette
lassee-<u>et</u>

la cuisinière
lah kweezeen-<u>yair</u>

l'évier
lev-e<u>eh</u>

Say the French word aloud.

la cuillère
lah kwee-<u>air</u>

la fourchette
lah foor-<u>shet</u>

À la campagne

Look for these words in the big picture.

l'arbre
larbr'

la fleur
lah fler

Find another bird in the book.

le champ
ler shom

la forêt
lah for<u>eh</u>

26

In the countryside

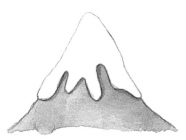

la montagne
lah mon<u>tyn</u>-y'

l'herbe
lairb

l'oiseau
lwuz-<u>oh</u>

le pont
ler pon

Say the French word aloud.

la rivière
lah reevee-<u>air</u>

27

L'heure du bain

Look for these words in the big picture.

le savon
ler sa<u>voh</u>

le lavabo
ler lava<u>boh</u>

la douche
lah doo<u>sh</u>

la serviette
lah sairvee-<u>et</u>

Find a bathroom on another page in the book.

Having a bath

les W.-C.
leh <u>doo</u>bl'veh seh

le miroir
ler meer<u>wah</u>

la brosse
à dents
lah bross
ah <u>dohn</u>

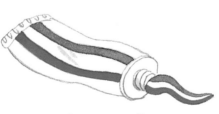

le dentifrice
ler dontee-<u>frees</u>

Say the French word aloud.

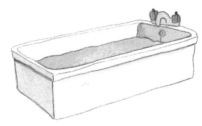

la baignoire
lah beyn-<u>nwah</u>

29

Dans ma chambre

Look for these words in the big picture.

le lit
ler lee

l'armoire
larm-<u>wah</u>

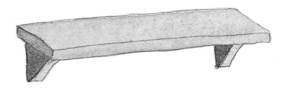

l'étagère
letah-<u>shair</u>

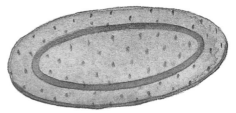

le tapis
ler tapee

Find a bed in another picture in the book.

30

In my bedroom

la télévision
lah teh-lehveezee<u>oh</u>

la fenêtre
lah f'<u>nair-tr</u>'

la porte
lah port

les chaussons
leh showss-<u>on</u>

le réveil
ler reh-<u>vay</u>

Say the French word aloud.

31

Ma maison

les toilettes
leh twah-<u>let</u>

la salle de bains
lah sal-der-<u>bah</u>

le plafond
ler plaf-<u>on</u>

la cuisine
la kwee-<u>zeen</u>

My house

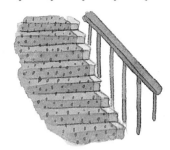

l'escalier
less-kalee-<u>eh</u>

le jardin
ler shar-<u>dah</u>

le toit
ler twah

le salon
ler sah-<u>loh</u>

Say the French word aloud.

la chambre
lah shombr'

33

Pendant la semaine

Look for these words in the big picture.

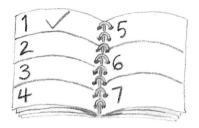

lundi
lern-dee

mardi
mar-dee

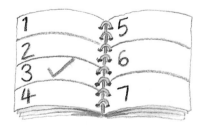

mercredi
mair-kr'-dee

jeudi
sher-dee

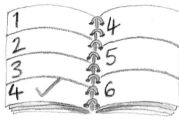

Say the French word aloud.

34

During the week

aujourd'hui
oh-shoor-<u>dwee</u>

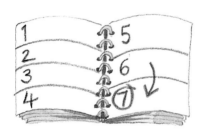

demain
der-<u>mah</u>

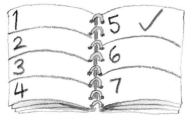

vendredi
<u>von</u>dr'-dee

samedi
<u>sam</u>dee

dimanche
<u>dee</u>-moh-nsh

35

Aller chez un ami

Look for these words in the big picture.

bonjour
boh-<u>shoor</u>

non
noh

oui
wee

s'il vous plaît
seel-voo-<u>pleh</u>

Say the French word aloud.

Visiting a friend

ça va
sa-_vah_

au revoir
oh-r'-_vwah_

merci
mair-_see_

voilà
vwah-lah

pardon
par-doh

Au parc

Look for these words in the big picture.

la fille
lah fee

la balançoire
lah balon-<u>swah</u>

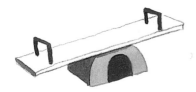

la bascule
lah bask-<u>yool</u>

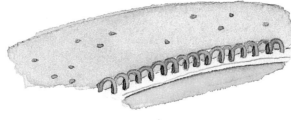

l'allée
lal-<u>eh</u>

Can you find a swan on another page?

At the park

le garçon
ler gar-<u>soh</u>

le banc
ler bon

le cerf-volant
ler sair-vo<u>loh</u>

l'enfant
lon<u>foh</u>

le lac
ler lack

Say the French word aloud.

Faire du sport

Look for these words in the big picture.

le ping-pong
ler peeng-<u>pong</u>

faire du ski
fair-doo-<u>skee</u>

Find other sports being played in the book.

la pêche
lah pesh

le football
ler foot<u>bol</u>

Playing sports

l'athlétisme
lat-leh-<u>tees</u>-m

faire du vélo
fair doo <u>vay</u>lo

nager
nah-<u>shay</u>

la gymnastique
lah jeem-nass-<u>teek</u>

Say the French word aloud.

le basket
ler bas<u>ket</u>

41

En ville

Look for these words in the big picture.

la maison
lah may-<u>zoh</u>

la gare
lah gaar

l'école
leh-<u>kol</u>

Find a picture that shows inside a school.

le supermarché
ler soo-pair-marsh-<u>ay</u>

In town

le marché
ler mar-<u>shay</u>

le magasin
ler mag-ah-<u>zah</u>

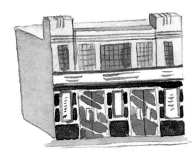

le cinéma
ler see-nay-<u>mah</u>

l'usine
l'yoo-<u>zeen</u>

la poste
lah post

Say the French word aloud.

43

Au supermarché

Look for these words in the big picture.

l'œuf
lerf

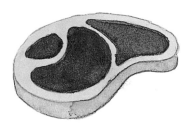

la viande
lah vee-<u>ond</u>

le pain
ler pah

le beurre
ler ber

Find milk on another page in the book.

44

At the supermarket

le riz
ler ree

le lait
ler lay

le sucre
ler s'<u>yoo</u>-kr'

le poisson
ler pwah-<u>son</u>

Say the French word aloud.

les pâtes
leh pat

45

Acheter des fruits

Look for these words in the big picture.

la pomme
lah pom

la pêche
la pesh

la cerise
lah seh-<u>reez</u>

l'ananas
lan-an-<u>ah</u>

Find some fruit in another picture.

Buying fruit

la banane
lah ban-*an*

le raisin
leh ray-*zah*

la fraise
lah frairz

l'orange
l*oronsh*

la mangue
lah *mon*-ger

Say the French word aloud.

47

Les contraires

Look for these words in the big picture.

court/courte
kor/kort

joli/jolie
shol-_ee_/shol-_ee_

grand/grande
groh/grond

cher/chère
share/share

petit/petite
p'-tee/p'-_teet_

heureux/heureuse

er-<u>er</u>/er-<u>erz</u>

triste

treest

bon/bonne

boh/bon

long/longue

loh/<u>lon</u>-ger

Say the French word aloud.

Quel temps fait-il?

Look for these words in the big picture.

le soleil
ler sol-_ay_

il fait chaud
eel fay <u>show</u>

il pleut
eel pler

Find some rain in another picture.

le nuage
ler noo-<u>ah</u>-sh

What's the weather like?

le vent
ler voh

il fait froid
eel fay <u>frwah</u>

il neige
eel <u>nair</u>-sh

l'orage
lor-<u>ah</u>-sh

le brouillard
ler brwee-<u>ar</u>

Say the French word aloud.

51

L'année – Le printemps et l'été

mars
marss

avril
av-<u>reel</u>

l'mai
may

la saison
lah say-<u>zoh</u>

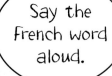

52

The year – Spring and summer

juin
sh-<u>wah</u>

juillet
<u>shwee</u>-ay

août
oot

These months are autumn and winter in the Southern Hemisphere!

le printemps
ler pran-<u>toh</u>

l'été
leh-<u>tay</u>

L'année – L'automne et l'hiver

Look for these words in the big picture.

septembre
sep-<u>tom</u>-br'

octobre
ok-<u>tobr</u>'

novembre
no-<u>vom</u>-br'

l'automne
lot-<u>on</u>

Say the French word aloud.

54

The year – Autumn and winter

décembre
deh-_som_-br'

janvier
shon-vee-ay

février
feh-vree-ay

l'hiver
lee-_vair_

le mois
ler mwah

These months are spring and summer in the Southern Hemisphere!

Cultiver des légumes

Look for these words in the big picture.

la pomme de terre
lah pom der <u>tair</u>

le maïs
ler my-<u>eess</u>

le chou
ler shoo

la carotte
la kah-<u>rot</u>

Say the French word aloud.

56

Growing vegetables

la tomate
lah to-<u>mat</u>

la laitue
lah layt-<u>yoo</u>

le céleri
ler sel-air-<u>ee</u>

la courgette
lah kor-<u>shet</u>

l'aubergine
loh-bair-<u>sheen</u>

Find vegetables in another picture in the book.

Dans la forêt

 Look for these words in the big picture.

l'écureuil
leh-koo<u>rer</u>-yee

la chenille
lah sher-<u>nee</u>-yer

le cerf
ler sairf

le scarabée
ler skah-rah-<u>bay</u>

 Find a butterfly in another picture.

58

In the forest

l'ours brun
loorss-<u>bruh</u>

le lapin
ler lah-<u>pah</u>

le papillon
ler papee-<u>oh</u>

le renard
ler ren-<u>ar</u>

la mouche
lah moosh

Say the French word aloud.

Les questions

Look for these words in the big picture.

qui ?
kee

qu'est-ce que ?
kess-<u>ker</u>

quand ?
koh

où ?
ooh

Can you think of another question?

Questions

ça va ?
sah vah

combien ?
kom-_bee_-ah

je peux ?
sh' perh

pourquoi ?
poor-kwah

comment ?
kom-_oh_

Say the French word aloud.

61

Vocabulaire

À la ferme p. 2	On the farm
le canard	duck
le chat	cat
le cheval	horse
la chèvre	goat
le chien	dog
le cochon	pig
le mouton	sheep
la souris	mouse
la vache	cow

Dans la salle de classe p. 4	In the classroom
la chaise	chair
la colle	glue
le crayon de couleur	coloured pencil
le livre	book
le papier	paper
la maîtresse	teacher
l'ordinateur	computer
le stylo	pen
la table	table

Ton corps p. 6	Your body
la bouche	mouth
le bras	arm
les épaules	shoulders
la jambe	leg
la main	hand
le nez	nose
le pied	foot
la tête	head
les yeux	eyes

Les couleurs dans la jungle p. 8	Colours in the jungle
blanc/blanche	white
bleu/bleue	blue
jaune	yellow
marron	brown
noir/noire	black
orange	orange
rouge	red
vert/verte	green
violet/violette	purple

Le coffre à déguisements p. 10	The dressing-up box
le chapeau	hat
les chaussettes	socks
les chaussures	shoes
la chemise	shirt
la jupe	skirt
le manteau	coat
le pantalon	trousers
le pyjama	pyjamas
la robe	dress

Au zoo p. 12	At the zoo
le crocodile	crocodile
le dauphin	dolphin
l'éléphant	elephant
la girafe	giraffe
l'hippopotame	hippopotamus
le lion	lion
l'ours blanc	polar bear
le serpent	snake
le tigre	tiger

Le transport p. 14	Transport
l'arrêt d'autobus	bus stop
l'autobus	bus
la bicyclette	bicycle
le camion	lorry
les feux	traffic lights
la rue	street
le trottoir	pavement
la voiture	car
la voiture de police	police car

À la plage p. 16	At the beach
les algues	seaweed
le coquillage	shell
la mer	sea
la mouette	seagull
le poisson	fish
le rocher	rock
le sable	sand
la vague	wave
le voilier	sailing boat

Ma famille p. 18	My family
mes cousins	cousins
mon frère	brother
ma grand-mère	grandmother
mon grand-père	grandfather
ma mère	mother
mon oncle	uncle
mon père	father
ma sœur	sister
ma tante	aunt

C'est la fête p. 20	Party time
le chocolat	chocolate
la boisson gazeuse	fizzy drink
l'eau	water
les frites	chips
le gâteau	cake
la glace	ice-cream
le jus d'orange	orange juice
la pizza	pizza
le sandwich	sandwich

Acheter des jouets p. 22	Shopping for toys
le baby-foot	table football
la balle	ball
le jeu	game
le jeu-vidéo	computer game
la maquette d'avion	model aeroplane kit
le nounours	teddy
les perles	beads
le puzzle	puzzle
le robot	robot

Dans la cuisine p. 24	In the kitchen
l'assiette	plate
la casserole	saucepan
le couteau	knife
la cuillère	spoon
la cuisinière	cooker
l'évier	sink
la fourchette	fork
le frigo	fridge
le verre	glass

À la campagne p. 26	In the countryside
l'arbre	tree
le champ	field
la fleur	flower
la forêt	forest
l'herbe	grass
la montagne	mountain
l'oiseau	bird
le pont	bridge
la rivière	river

L'heure du bain p. 28	Bathtime
la baignoire	bath
la brosse à dents	toothbrush
les W.-C.	toilet
le dentifrice	toothpaste
la douche	shower
le lavabo	washbasin
le miroir	mirror
le savon	soap
la serviette	towel

Dans ma chambre p. 30	In my bedroom
l'armoire	wardrobe
l'étagère	shelf
la fenêtre	window
le lit	bed
la porte	door
le réveil	alarm clock
le tapis	rug
la télévision	television
les chaussons	slippers

Word list

Ma maison p.32	My house
les toilettes	toilet
la cuisine	kitchen
la salle de bains	bathroom
l'escalier	stairs
la chambre	bedroom
le jardin	garden
le salon	sitting room
le plafond	ceiling
le toit	roof

Les jours de la semaine p.34	Days of the week
lundi	Monday
mardi	Tuesday
mercredi	Wednesday
jeudi	Thursday
vendredi	Friday
samedi	Saturday
dimanche	Sunday
aujourd'hui	today
demain	tomorrow

Aller chez un ami p.36	Visiting a friend
au revoir	goodbye
merci	thanks
bonjour	hello
non	no
ça va	that's okay
pardon	sorry
s'il vous plaît	please
oui	yes
voilà	here you are

Au parc p.38	At the park
la bascule	see-saw
le banc	bench
l'allée	path
la balançoire	swing
le cerf-volant	kite
le lac	lake
le garçon	boy
l'enfant	child
la fille	girl

Faire du sport p.40	Playing sports
l'athlétisme	athletics
le basket	basketball
faire du ski	skiing
faire du vélo	cycling
le football	football
la gymnastique	gymnastics
nager	swimming
la pêche	fishing
le ping-pong	table tennis

En ville p.42	In town
le cinéma	cinema
l'école	school
la gare	station
le magasin	shop
la maison	house
le marché	market
la poste	post office
le supermarché	supermarket
l'usine	factory

Au supermarché p.44	At the supermarket
le beurre	butter
le lait	milk
l'œuf	egg
le pain	bread
les pâtes	pasta
le poisson	fish
le riz	rice
le sucre	sugar
la viande	meat

Acheter des fruits p.46	Buying fruit
l'ananas	pineapple
la banane	banana
la cerise	cherry
la fraise	strawberry
la mangue	mango
l'orange	orange
la pêche	peach
la pomme	apple
le raisin	grapes

Les contraires p.48	Opposites
joli/jolie	pretty
bon/bonne	good
cher/chère	expensive
court/courte	short
grand/grande	happy
heureux/heureuse	big
long/longue	long
petit/petite	small
triste	sad

Quel temps fait-il? p.50	What's the weather like?
le brouillard	fog
il fait chaud	it's hot
il fait froid	it's cold
il neige	it's snowing
le nuage	cloud
l'orage	storm
il pleut	it's raining
le soleil	sun
le vent	wind

L'année p.52 Le printemps et l'été	The year Spring and summer
la saison	season
le printemps	spring
mars	March
avril	April
mai	May
l'été	summer
juin	June
juillet	July
août	August

L'année p.54 L'automne et l'hiver	The year Autumn and winter
l'automne	autumn
septembre	September
octobre	October
novembre	November
l'hiver	winter
décembre	December
janvier	January
février	February
le mois	month

Cultiver des légumes p.56	Growing vegetables
l'aubergine	aubergine
la carotte	carrot
le céleri	celery
le chou	cabbage
la courgette	courgette
la laitue	lettuce
le maïs	corn
la pomme de terre	potato
la tomate	tomato

Dans la forêt p.58	In the forest
le cerf	deer
la chenille	caterpillar
l'écureuil	squirrel
le lapin	rabbit
la mouche	fly
l'ours brun	brown bear
le papillon	butterfly
le renard	fox
le scarabée	beetle

Les questions p.60	Questions
combien ?	how many?
ça va ?	how are you?
comment ?	how?
où ?	where?
pourquoi ?	why?
je peux ?	can I?
quand ?	when?
qu'est-ce que ?	what?
qui ?	who?

Answers

Page 2
There is another cat on pages 24, 29 and 44.

Page 4
There are other chairs on pages 18, 19, 25, 31 and 32.

Page 6
There are 12 children at the party.

Page 8
There are three purple things in the scene.

Page 10
There is someone wearing a hat on pages 8, 16, 20, 40, 44, 46, 48, 51, 53, 55, 56, 60 and 61.

Page 12
There are other animals that could be in a zoo on pages 8, 55 and 58.

Page 14
There is a car on page 34.

Page 16
There are fish on pages 45 and 46.

Page 20
There are balloons on pages 6 and 7.

Page 22
There is a teddy bear on page 30 and on page 33.

Page 24
There are glasses on pages 18, 20, 21, 36 and 37.

Page 26
There are birds on pages 2, 8, 16, 17, 26, 32, 39, 46 and 52.

Page 28
There is a bathroom on page 32.

Page 30
There is a bed on page 32.

Page 32
There is a house on pages 2 and 35.

Page 38
There is a swan on page 27.

Page 40
There are sports being played on pages 34 and 50.

Page 42
There is a picture that shows inside a school on pages 4 and 5.

Page 44
There is milk on page 24.

Page 46
There is fruit on pages 15, 18 and 24.

Page 50
There is rain on pages 52 and 53.

Page 56
There are vegetables on pages 18, 21 and 35.

Page 58
There is a butterfly on pages 8, 9 and 26.

Published by b small publishing ltd.
www.bsmall.co.uk
Text and illustrations © b small publishing ltd. 2018
1 2 3 4 5   ISBN 978-1-911509-41-7
Design: Louise Millar   Production: Madeleine Ehm   Language adviser: Marie-Thérèse Bougard   Publisher: Sam Hutchinson   Editorial: Sam Hutchinson
Printed in China by WKT Co. Ltd.

British Library Cataloguing-in-Publication Data.
A catalogue record for this book is available from the British Library.